THE CIVIL WAR

RIVER TO VICTORY

The Civil War in the West 1861-1863

James R. Arnold and Roberta Wiener

LERNER PUBLICATIONS COMPANY • MINNEAPOLIS

**First American edition published in 2002
by Lerner Publications Company**

© 2002 by Lerner Publications Company

The Civil War series is created and produced by Graham Beehag Books, in cooperation with Lerner Publications Company, a division of Lerner Publishing Group.

Lerner Publications Company
A division of Lerner Publishing Group
241 First Avenue North
Minneapolis, Minnesota 55401 U.S.A.

Website address: www.lernerbooks.com

Library of Congress Cataloging-in-Publication Data

Arnold, James R.
  River to victory : the Civil War in the West 1861-1863 / by James R. Arnold and Roberta Wiener.
       p. cm.—(The Civil War)
Includes bibliographical references and index.
  ISBN 0-8225-2314-0 (lib. bdg. : alk. paper)
  1. Southwest, Old—History—Civil War, 1861-1865—Campaigns—Juvenile literature. 2. Tennessee—History—Civil War, 1861-1865—Campaigns—Juvenile literature. 3. Kentucky—History—Civil War, 1861-1865—Campaigns—Juvenile literature. 4. Mississippi River Valley—History—Civil War, 1861-1865—Campaigns—Juvenile literature. I. Wiener, Roberta. II. Title. III. Civil War (Minneapolis, Minn.)
  E470.4 .A76   2001
  973.7'3'0976—dc21   00-013123

Printed in Singapore
Bound in the United States of America
1 2 3 4 5 6 – OS – 07 06 05 04 03 02

Front cover picture: In April 1863, during the Vicksburg campaign in Mississippi, Union ships break through a Confederate blockade on the Mississippi River.

Back cover picture: General Ulysses S. Grant poses with his staff at army headquarters.

Contents

WORDS YOU NEED TO KNOW

advance: to move forward toward the enemy army

base: a place where an army or navy keeps its food and supplies

bombard: to fire artillery (cannons and other large guns) at a target, such as a fort

campaign: a series of military actions, such as marches and battles, to capture a certain place

earthworks: walls made of dirt that protect soldiers on a battlefield

flank: one side of a group of soldiers

fleet: a group of ships that moves and fights together

infantry: soldiers who move and fight on foot

mortar: a type of cannon that shoots high into the air

musket: a type of gun used by foot soldiers before rifles became commonly used. Muskets were not as accurate as rifles in hitting a target.

neutral: not taking a side

occupy: to enter and take control of an enemy fort or town

rebel: the nickname used by Northerners to refer to the citizens of the Southern states, who were in rebellion against the United States

regular army: the standing army that is kept ready for a war, even during times of peace. Regular soldiers are professional soldiers—being in the army is their job.

reinforcements: soldiers sent into a battle, after it has begun, to help their side win

retreat: to turn back, or away from, a battle

surrender: to stop fighting and give in to the other side

theater: a large geographical area in which the battles of a war take place

Yankee: the Southern nickname for the citizens of the Northern states

Moving on from Virginia

The Northern states and the Southern states had been growing apart for many years. They disagreed about whether slavery was right or wrong. They also disagreed about whether the Southern states had the right to leave the United States of America. In 1861, the Southern states formed their own nation: the Confederate States of America, also called the Confederacy. Citizens of this new nation called themselves Confederates. The Confederates believed that they had to fight the North to win their independence. Northerners called the Southerners rebels, because the South had rebelled, or revolted, against the North. Southerners called all Northerners Yankees, after the popular name for people who lived in the New England states. Northerners called their states the Union. They wanted to keep both Northern and Southern states unified, or together, as one nation. And Northerners were willing to fight to accomplish this goal. So the war began.

The first major Civil War battles took place in the east, when Union and Confederate armies met in Virginia. The North wanted to win the war by capturing the capital city of the Confederacy: Richmond, Virginia. At the same time, the North needed to protect its own capital: Washington, D.C.

The first battles proved to both sides that they could no longer hope for the war to end quickly. These battles also showed that the generals and soldiers on both sides had a lot to learn about how to fight a war. President Abraham Lincoln of the Union and President Jefferson Davis of the Confederacy struggled to find the right generals to lead their armies. Meanwhile, the Civil War soon spread west to places far away from the capital cities.

CHAPTER ONE

The Western Theater

The Civil War was fought in two major theaters, or geographical areas: Virginia in the east and the Mississippi-Tennessee River region in the west.

Everyone understood why the eastern theater was important. Both capital cities—Washington and Richmond—were in the east. Neither the North nor the South could afford to lose its capital. At the beginning of the war, Lincoln and Davis did not think the west was as important as the east.

But the west was important. In order to win the Civil War, both sides had to fight for control of both theaters, not just the eastern one. In the west, the important fighting took place between the Mississippi River and the Allegheny Mountains. This was a large area compared to where the fighting took place in the east.

The "White House of the Confederacy," below, where Jefferson Davis lived in Richmond, Virginia, while he was the Confederate president

The major rivers of the west served as highways for moving people and goods.

In addition to its size, the western theater differed from the eastern theater in two major ways. First, the western theater had fewer big cities and fewer railroads than the east. This made it harder for western armies to get supplies such as food and ammunition. Second, the flow of the rivers in the west was different than in the east. In the east, the major rivers flowed from west to east. These rivers formed a natural barrier that helped stop Union soldiers from marching south. In the west, the major rivers flowed north and south. This gave the Union natural avenues (routes) to follow to invade the South. During the first years of the war, most fighting in the west took place on and along these natural avenues.

During the Civil War, the Union government formed the U.S. Military Railroads (USMRR) to move soldiers, weapons, and supplies to where they were needed. A new engine built by the USMRR, below

A mob of Confederate supporters throwing rocks at Union soldiers in Saint Louis, Missouri

The Border States

When the war began, both sides tried to control the states of Missouri and Kentucky, which were on the border between the North and the South. No one knew which way Missouri would go. Most people in the southern half of the state supported the Confederacy. Many in the northern half supported the Union.

A fierce political battle took place. A determined Union officer (a military rank that makes a soldier a leader) named Nathaniel Lyon managed to hold Missouri in the Union. Lyon did this by capturing a group of rebels before they could steal Union weapons. Most Missouri rebels left the state to join rebel soldiers in other places.

Lyon's success was important. It allowed Saint Louis, Missouri, to serve as a major Union base (place that provides food and supplies for an army or navy). Also, Union control of Missouri secured, or made safe, the Union flank.

Armies most easily pay attention to what is happening in front of them. It is harder for an army to pay attention to what is happening on their right and left flanks, or sides. An enemy force, or group of soldiers, on the right or left flank is dangerous. Union control of Missouri let Union armies move south without having to worry about the Union right flank.

Kentucky also had a fierce political conflict. Kentucky's political leaders sharply disagreed about whether to support the North or the South. In the end, Kentucky decided not to support either side. In other words, Kentucky stayed neutral.

Neither the Union nor the Confederacy wanted to be the first to enter Kentucky and violate, or disturb, its neutrality. But Kentucky was like a great shield protecting the western Confederacy. If the Union army took control of Kentucky, Union soldiers could move farther south. If the Union forces could not enter Kentucky, they had only one other way to invade the South. That way was to move south down the Mississippi River.

Confederate leaders worried that the Union might use the Mississippi River to invade the South. On September 3, 1861, a Confederate force moved into Kentucky to occupy (take control of) Columbus, an important town on the Mississippi River. The Confederates did this because there was high ground at Columbus. High ground is always useful to soldiers. From the top of a hill, soldiers can see farther and shoot better at their enemy. The rebels wanted to build

a fort on this high ground to block any Union ships from moving south down the river.

This move was a mistake for the South. The Confederates had just violated Kentucky's neutrality, so the Union forces felt free to do the

The Confederates placed guns like these along the Mississippi River and other waterways so soldiers could aim at any Union boats that tried to pass by.

ULYSSES S. GRANT

Hiram Ulysses Grant was born in Ohio in 1822. He disliked working in his father's tannery (leather-making shop) and loved to be outdoors and ride horses. He reluctantly attended the U.S. Military Academy at West Point because it was his only chance to get more education. He earned just average grades, except in math and horseback riding. He graduated in 1843. Somebody made a mistake and registered him at the academy as Ulysses S. Grant. Grant decided to keep the new middle initial. His nickname was Sam. Later in life, he decided to make the "S" stand for Simpson, his mother's maiden name.

Grant fought in the Mexican War and received recognition for his bravery. After the war, in 1848, he married Julia Dent. They had four children. His army duties took him away from his family. He resigned from, or left, the army in 1854 because he missed his family. But many said he resigned because he got into trouble for drinking too much alcohol. Grant tried to make a living from farming and business in Illinois. But he failed and went to work in his father's leather business.

Throughout his life, Grant did not make a good impression when people first met him. He was small, dressed poorly, and didn't have much to say. But the more people got to know Grant, the more they respected him for his modesty and firmness. When he first arrived to take over the rough and rude soldiers of the 21st Illinois Volunteers during the Civil War, all he said to them was, "I guess I've come to take command." When the men made fun of him, he was able to quiet them with a steady stare. Grant became a good leader because he understood that enemy soldiers were more afraid of him than he was of them.

same. On September 5, 1861, a Union force entered Kentucky to occupy the key town of Paducah. Control of Paducah let the Union control parts of both the Ohio River and the Mississippi River, and the entrance to the Tennessee River. The Union officer who made this move did it without orders. He had plenty of common sense and knew that controlling Paducah was a good idea. His name was Ulysses S. Grant.

After General Grant captured Paducah, other Union soldiers poured over the Ohio River and into Kentucky. Suddenly, the Confederacy's shield was gone. Tennessee, the heartland of the Confederacy, was open to attack. The Union could strike anywhere from the Mississippi River to the mountains of eastern Tennessee.

President Davis sent a general named Albert Sidney Johnston to meet this Northern threat. Johnston had graduated from the U.S. Military Academy at West Point and had fought in the Mexican War (1846–1848). More important, he was also Davis's trusted friend. Johnston's small Confederate army advanced (marched forward) north into Kentucky to meet the Union forces. His advance frightened Northern commanders. They stopped their advance south.

Union soldiers rally to defend Kentucky. These men do not have uniforms and one carries an umbrella.

13

A *Union soldier*, above, *with his blanket rolled up, which was the most comfortable way to carry it*

A *Union corporal*, above

When a new company of volunteer Union soldiers formed, below, they were proud to receive their own flag.

But Johnston knew that his Confederate army could be attacked by a larger Union army. He asked Davis to send reinforcements, or extra soldiers. But at this time, the Confederacy faced many threats, especially in Virginia. Confederate generals everywhere were asking Davis for help. Davis replied to Johnston, "Where am I to get arms [weapons] and men?"

During the rest of 1861, both sides taught their armies how to fight. Most of the new soldiers were civilians who volunteered to fight. They believed that it was their duty to serve their country. Boys from states such as Ohio, Indiana, Illinois, Michigan, and Wisconsin eagerly volunteered to serve in the Union army. They had little idea of what war really was.

The Confederate volunteers who served in the west came from Tennessee, Alabama, Mississippi, and nearby states. They matched the Union boys in courage and determination. But they, too, had little experience of war.

Most western soldiers, whether Union or Confederate, were stubborn fighters. They did not give up easily. When western armies met on the battlefield, soldiers fought with amazing courage. Stubbornness and courage meant that the battles in the west were fierce and bloody.

Confederate soldiers in camp. Early in the war, few had uniforms.

15

CHAPTER TWO

The North Finds a General

A military campaign is a series of moves, or marches, that lead soldiers toward a goal. The campaign season began in February 1862 when the weather began to warm up. The commander of the western Union armies, Major General Henry Halleck, ordered General Grant to advance southeast along the natural avenue of the Tennessee River. A rebel fort named Fort Henry blocked this river. Grant's job was to capture it. In order to do this, Grant planned to work with the ships of the Union navy.

The North had many more ships and sailors than the South. Confederates relied on forts, rather than ships, to defend Southern rivers.

A Northern naval architect named Samuel Pook designed ironclads to attack Confederate forts. Ironclads were giant ships with sloping iron sides, which caused shots to bounce off. The ironclads'

The sides of an ironclad, above, *were sloped so cannonballs would bounce off.*

Workers at Union shipyards in places such as Saint Louis, below, built the ironclads and other boats that served in the west.

thickest armor was at the front. This armor let them fight while pointed directly at enemy forts.

The Union navy hired an inventor-engineer named James B. Eads to build the ironclads that Pook had designed. Eads promised to finish the job

A Union ship under construction, left. *Waterproofing the wood is one of the important steps in shipbuilding.*

Cannons being made in an iron foundry, opposite. *The Fort Pitt Works in Pittsburgh, Pennsylvania,* below, *where cannons were made for the Union's ironclad ships.*

in sixty-three days or less. It seemed an impossible promise. To make it come true, Eads hired eight hundred men who worked day and night. He personally kept the work moving ahead by finding everything needed to build the ironclads.

The rapid construction of the ironclads showed the strength of Northern industry. However, when the ships were done, they did not look like anything anyone in the west had ever seen. People called the ironclads "Pook's turtles" because the

THE FT PITT WORKS FROM THE RIVER, PITTSBURGH PA

Ironclads like the USS Cairo, left, *had very thick armor at the front so they could withstand up close battles against enemy forts on narrow rivers.*

ships moved slowly and the armor reminded them of a turtle's shell. Many people wondered if the ironclads would work.

The test came on February 6, 1862. General Grant made a plan with navy commander Andrew Foote to capture Fort Henry. To begin, Foote led his ironclads in an attack against the fort. Earth walls fourteen feet thick protected the Confederate gunners inside the fort. Armor plating several inches thick protected the Union sailors inside the ironclads. Both sides fired their cannons furiously. Foote's ship suffered at least thirty hits. Another ironclad received seventy-two hits.

But Fort Henry was on low ground. The Confederates could not defend their fort against the Union ships. After an eighty-minute fight, Fort Henry surrendered, or gave up.

Foote called it "a good day's work." But Grant wanted more. He wrote to his wife to say that in two days he would march east and attack the Confederate Fort Donelson.

Union ironclads bombard Fort Henry, below.

On to Fort Donelson

Just as Fort Henry blocked the Tennessee River, Fort Donelson blocked the Cumberland River. Grant wanted to advance quickly against it before the Confederates could send reinforcements. A newspaper reporter asked him if he knew about the Confederate strength at Fort Donelson. Grant answered that he did not, but that he still thought his army could take the fort.

Very few generals would have taken such a risk. Grant's Union army was in the Confederate state of Tennessee, deep in enemy territory. The Union army's back was to a major river, at a spot where no bridges went across it. If Grant's army had to retreat (move back), his soldiers would not be able to cross the river. It was winter, and the army had no tents or camp equipment. Grant boldly ordered his army to advance toward Fort Donelson anyway.

Iowa soldiers cross a small river during a march in Tennessee.

The USS St. Louis *was the first ironclad gunboat built by James B. Eads.*

The march began on February 12, 1862. It happened to be a warm day. The Union boys thought that it was always like this in the "sunny South." They were not prepared when winter returned as they marched toward Fort Donelson. An Iowa soldier wrote to his mother: "Just as we halted [stopped] it commenced [started] raining and we huddled down as best we could, one of the boys and my self got down on a bunch of wet leaves and covered our blankets over us. But we had not laid very long before the rain [ended] and it grew cold and it commenced snowing—I tell you it was cold. I shaked like I had the [fever]."

Grant's army of 25,000 soldiers surrounded Fort Donelson. A Confederate force of 15,000 men was inside the fort. The Union army waited for the Union navy to make the first attack. On February 14, Foote attacked the fort with his Union ironclads. Everyone expected the navy to win another victory.

The view seen by Confederate gunners at Fort Donelson, left, when they looked down the Cumberland River

But Fort Donelson's guns were in a good position on high ground. A Union officer aboard one of the ironclads described what took place: "As we drew nearer, the enemy's fire greatly increased in force and effect. . . . We heard the deafening crack of the bursting shells, the crash of solid shot, and the whizzing of fragments of shell and wood as they sped through the [ironclad]. Soon a 128-pounder [solid iron ball] struck our anchor, smashed it into flying bolts. . . . Another ripped up the iron plating. . . and still they came, harder and faster, taking flag-staffs and smoke-stacks, and tearing off the side armor as lightning tears the bark from a tree."

The Confederate guns badly hurt the ironclads. Eleven Union sailors were killed and forty-three wounded. Foote himself was wounded. The Union navy had tried and failed. Grant realized that he had no choice but to lay siege to, or attack, the fort with his infantry (soldiers who fight on foot). Meanwhile, his hungry men shivered in the cold wind as the temperature fell to twelve degrees.

Unconditional Surrender

Inside Fort Donelson, the Confederates were cold and discouraged. The rebels knew that they were surrounded. The situation seemed hopeless. The fort's commander was General John B. Floyd. Before the war, Floyd had been a powerful political leader. He was a good politician but a bad general. He did not know what to do.

Floyd called a meeting with his generals. They decided to try to fight their way out of the fort and retreat southeast toward Nashville, Tennessee.

The plan had a good chance of working. Grant and his men did not expect an attack. The Union forces had left their right flank unprotected. The rebels began a surprise attack against the Union's right flank at daybreak on February 15, 1862.

A typical group of tough Union soldiers in the west, below

AN ILLINOIS COMPANY AT WAR

Ninety-nine men made up Company C, 8th Illinois Volunteers at Fort Donelson. They were all country boys. Half were under twenty-two years old, eight were over thirty. Only two soldiers were born outside the United States: one in England and one in Ireland. Three out of every four were farmers. Sixty-seven of seventy-eight privates (soldiers of the lowest rank) were unmarried. The battle was so fierce on February 15, 1862, that by the next morning only seventeen men were still able to report for duty (show up to fight again).

Hard fighting began. Union General Lew Wallace commanded a division (a large group of several thousand soldiers) that fought against the rebel attack. He wrote that the noise of muskets (guns) firing was so loud that it sounded "as if a million men were beating empty barrels with iron hammers."

After several hours of fighting, the rebels fought their way past the Union soldiers. A Confederate cavalry force (soldiers on horseback) led by Colonel Nathan Bedford Forrest fought especially well. By noon, Floyd's men had won an escape route.

Riders galloped to Grant's headquarters to report the disaster. But Grant was away at a meeting with Foote and the Union navy. When Grant learned that his soldiers were fighting, he galloped to the battle. He found many of his men running away. Only a few units (small groups of soldiers) were still fighting.

Battle of Fort Donelson

27

Grant learned that the rebels had attacked while carrying full knapsacks (backpacks). He correctly guessed that this meant they were trying to escape from Fort Donelson. He told an aide that his men seemed demoralized, or discouraged. But he also thought that the Confederates must be badly disorganized from the fighting. Victory, he said, would go to the army that attacked next. He said that the enemy "will have to hurry if he gets ahead of me."

Grant reacted to the crisis with firmness. He did not think of giving up. On the Confederate side,

When soldiers fought in the forest, they could barely see the enemy because of the smoke and trees.

The inner defenses at Fort Donelson

Floyd hesitated, became confused, and held several more discussions with his generals. He finally ordered his men to retreat back to the fort.

The situation had changed by the time the rebels returned to the fort. One Union division had not yet fought. It was led by a tough, experienced, sixty-year-old regular (professional) army soldier named C. F. Smith. Smith was good with his men. He led by example. One young soldier wrote, "I was scared to death, but I saw the old man's white moustache. . . and went on."

Smith was not completely happy with his men. He shouted out, "I see skulkers [men trying to avoid fighting], I'll have none here. Come on, you volunteers, come on. This is your chance. You volunteered to be killed for love of country and

29

now you can be!" Smith's division captured part of Fort Donelson.

That night, Floyd held another meeting with his generals. He decided there was nothing to do but to surrender. Floyd himself was a coward. He escaped from Fort Donelson aboard a steamboat. He left his men behind to become prisoners.

One Confederate officer refused to let his men become prisoners. Colonel Forrest led his cavalry to safety. His men made a night march along an old, abandoned road. By refusing to accept defeat, Forrest and his men lived to fight another day.

On February 16, 1862, the commander at Fort Donelson asked Grant for surrender terms. Such terms were a formal

Colonel Nathan Bedford Forrest, above, *joined the Confederate army as a private. By the end of the Civil War, he had been promoted to the high rank of lieutenant general.*

A Confederate earthwork (wall of dirt) that protected Confederate soldiers at Fort Donelson, right

military agreement about how the prisoners and their equipment would be treated. Grant replied with words that quickly became famous throughout the North. He would accept "no terms except unconditional and immediate surrender."

About 11,500 Confederates surrendered along with forty artillery pieces (cannons and other large guns). It was a great Union victory and a bad Confederate defeat.

The initials for Grant's name were U. S. (Ulysses Simpson). Newspaper reporters wrote that the U. S. stood for "Unconditional Surrender" Grant. At this time in the Civil War, the North badly needed a hero. Grant's victories at Fort Henry and Fort Donelson made him this hero.

Union General U. S. Grant received the unconditional surrender of Fort Donelson at this hotel in Dover, Tennessee.

Chapter Three

Bloody Shiloh

Grant's victories opened the way for a Union invasion of Tennessee. The Confederate situation was desperate. Confederate General Albert Sidney Johnston ordered a retreat south from Kentucky. Some Southerners criticized this decision. They did not like it when any Confederate general gave up Confederate territory. Johnston knew that his strategy (military plan) to retreat was the right thing to do. Grant and his Union army had already moved past him into Tennessee. But he also understood the Southern people. He realized that "what the people want is a battle and a victory," not a retreat.

In Richmond, political leaders from Tennessee asked President Davis to remove Johnston. They said that he "was no general." Davis replied that if Johnston was not a general, "we had better give up the war, for we have no general."

Another Confederate general named Braxton Bragg made a suggestion. He said that the Confederate forces were too scattered, or spread out. He recommended moving soldiers away from unimportant places and sending the men to Tennessee. Davis knew that this was taking a big risk. If he ordered men to leave a place, the Yankees might attack and capture it. But Grant's victories gave him no choice.

Trains rushed rebel soldiers to western Tennessee from places as far away as Mobile, Alabama, and New Orleans, Louisiana. The

Confederate troops camped at Corinth, Mississippi, before their attack on Grant's Union army, which was camped about twenty miles away in Tennessee.

reinforcements gave Johnston about 40,000 men. Johnston decided to attack Grant's army.

By this time, Grant had moved his army to Pittsburg Landing on the Tennessee River. In peaceful times, steamboats stopped at Pittsburg Landing to unload their cargo. Grant's 33,000 men spread out around Pittsburg Landing, rested, and drilled (practiced for battle). They believed that the rebels were far away.

Union troops were transported by steamboat down the Tennessee River.

The Battle of Shiloh

On April 5, 1862, the Confederate army deployed, or lined up, for battle. Johnston's plan depended on two things: surprising the Union army, and striking before Union reinforcements arrived. Some of the Confederate generals became nervous. General Pierre Beauregard suggested a retreat. Johnston disagreed. He said the attack would begin at dawn the next day.

Meanwhile, the Union soldiers had no idea that they were in danger. They were camped in a bad spot. Thick forests filled the area. The soldiers could not see their surroundings very well because trees blocked their view.

Behind them was the Tennessee River. The river had no bridges across it, and the water was too deep for the soldiers to walk through. If they had to retreat, they would be trapped against the river.

At first light on April 6, the rebel advance began. Johnston got on his horse and told his soldiers, "Tonight we will water our horses [let our horses drink] in the Tennessee River." The fierce attack surprised the Union soldiers in their camps. A reporter described the scene: "Some, particularly among our officers, were not yet out of bed. Others were dressing, others washing, others cooking, a few eating their breakfasts."

Pierre Gustave Toutant Beauregard, above, second in command at Shiloh, was admired as a Confederate general. In fact, two foreign countries offered him jobs commanding their armies after the Civil War.

Union soldiers relaxed in camp, left, during the days before the Confederate surprise attack at Shiloh.

Union General William Tecumseh Sherman, above, was wounded at Shiloh but stayed on the battlefield and kept fighting.

Union soldiers from Indiana fire blindly into the smoke during the Battle of Shiloh, below.

Confederates came rushing out of the woods. General William T. Sherman commanded a Union division that met the first attack. His men had never been in a battle before. Even though they were surprised by the attack, many Union soldiers formed a line and fired their muskets. Others ran away in terror.

No one could see what was going on because the trees and musket smoke blocked their view. Officers on both sides simply sent more men toward the sounds of the heaviest firing. Slowly the Confederates pushed back the Union soldiers. Behind the Union line was Pittsburg Landing and the Tennessee River. If the Confederates could advance all the way to Pittsburg Landing, they would trap the Union soldiers at the river and win the battle. Johnston's promise to let his horse drink from the Tennessee River looked like it might come true.

The fighting was most fierce around an area that became known as the "Hornets' Nest." This was a low-lying dirt road blocking the Confederate advance to Pittsburg Landing. In order to capture the Hornets' Nest, the attackers had to move across open farm fields. A Union soldier from Illinois described what he saw: "The Confederate line of battle was in plain sight. It was in the open, in the edge of an old field. . . . Even the ramrods [used to load the muskets] could be seen flashing in the air."

Grant ordered his men to keep control of the Hornets'

Nest at all costs. During a five-hour period, twelve separate Confederate attacks struck the Hornets' Nest. Some of the attackers got within twenty yards of the defending line before the defenders fought them back. One rebel soldier wrote how the defenders "mow [cut] us down" every time the Union soldiers fired. So many wounded and dead Confederates fell to the ground that the area looked like a "slaughter pen."

Johnston believed that his soldiers needed encouragement. To set a good example, he bravely rode among them and was often very close to the fighting. He even led one attack against the Hornets' Nest. His courage cost him his life. He received a serious wound and bled to death. General Beauregard took Johnston's place.

Finally the Confederates shot all their cannons at once against the defenders. A terrific bombardment, or artillery fire, took place. At the same time, rebel soldiers moved around the sides

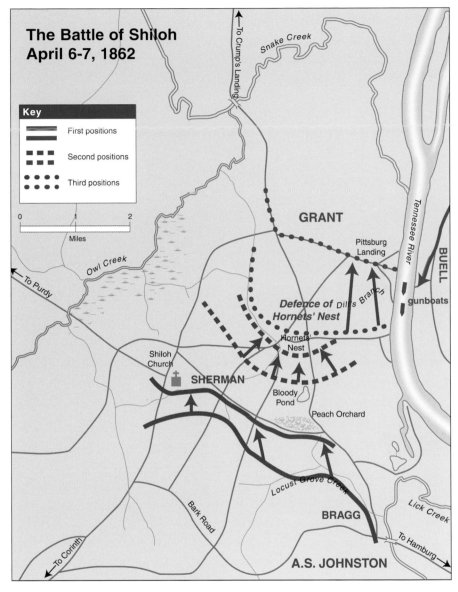

The Battle of Shiloh April 6-7, 1862

Key
First positions
Second positions
Third positions

0   1   2
Miles

To Crump's Landing
Snake Creek
GRANT
Pittsburg Landing
Tennessee River
BUELL
gunboats
Owl Creek
To Purdy
Defence of Dill's Branch Hornets' Nest
Hornets' Nest
Shiloh Church
SHERMAN
Bloody Pond
Peach Orchard
Locust Grove Creek
Bark Road
BRAGG
Lick Creek
To Hamburg
To Corinth
A.S. JOHNSTON

of the Hornets' Nest. At about 5:30 P.M., 2,200 surviving Union soldiers surrendered the Hornets' Nest to the Confederates. Their brave fight, even though they lost, gave the rest of Grant's army time to prepare for one more fight.

By dark, the Confederates had almost reached the Tennessee River. Thousands of scared Union soldiers were hiding along the river. A Union officer shouted to them, "Fall in, boys, fall in and follow me! We shall whip [beat] them yet!" The soldiers did not budge. They had seen many men die. They did not want to fight anymore.

If Johnston were alive, he might have gotten the Confederates to try again to reach the river and win the battle. But the Confederates were exhausted, hungry, and disorganized. A few tried a last attack. But during the night, 25,000 more Union reinforcements came to Pittsburg Landing. Most belonged to General

The defense of the Hornets' Nest

Don Carlos Buell's army. The next day the Union forces attacked. After hard fighting, the Union soldiers drove the rebels from the battlefield.

The battle became known as the Battle of Shiloh, after the nearby Shiloh church. It was the Civil War's bloodiest battle so far. The total Union loss of killed, wounded, and captured soldiers was close to 13,700. The Confederate loss was 10,700. The high number of losses shocked people in the North.

Some people thought the Union had been surprised at Shiloh and lost so many soldiers because Grant had been drunk. At one time, Grant had had a drinking problem. But he was not drunk at Shiloh. In Washington, D.C., some politicians

After the Battle of Shiloh, soldiers burn some of the hundreds of dead horses, above.

The 9th Illinois, a group of Union soldiers, fought so well at Shiloh, opposite, *they were praised by Confederate General Albert Sidney Johnston.*

Frightened Union soldiers run back to safety at Pittsburg Landing, right.

urged Lincoln to fire Grant. Lincoln replied, "I can't spare [do without] this man; he fights."

The South had done everything it could to destroy Grant's army. Even with the advantages of surprise and more men, the Confederates had failed. President Davis's favorite general, Albert Sidney Johnston, had died in the battle. Later, Davis remarked, "When Sidney Johnston fell, it was the turning point of our fate; for we had no other to take up his work in the West."

Both sides were exhausted by the Battle of Shiloh. The Confederates retreated south to Corinth, Mississippi. The Union men rested at Shiloh. For those who had fought the Battle of Shiloh, war had lost all of its glory.

CHAPTER FOUR

Battles along the Mississippi River

Grant's battles were only one part of the bigger Union strategy. This strategy called for taking control of the Mississippi River by attacking it from both ends. The Confederate fort at Columbus, Kentucky, blocked the upper end of the great river. Its guns would shoot at any Union ships that tried to move past it. Two forts located south of New Orleans blocked the lower end.

New Orleans was the South's biggest city. It was one of the few places in the South with great industrial workshops. It had skilled workers capable of building wooden and iron-sided ships. Workers began building powerful ironclads to defend the city. Until the ironclads were finished, New Orleans depended on two old forts to protect it.

The forts were about ninety miles southeast of the city. Fort St. Philip sat on the river's east bank, or side. Fort Jackson was across the river on the west bank. Together, the forts had about eighty cannons aiming at the water. The Confederates sank many old ships in the river to make a barrier that stretched between the forts. A heavy chain floated on top of them. This barrier blocked Union ships from moving toward New Orleans.

A small Confederate fleet, or group of ships, helped protect the forts. This fleet included some partially finished ironclads. The Confederate defense appeared very strong and ready to protect New Orleans.

New Orleans in 1862

During February and March of 1862, a Union fleet gathered to attack. The fleet's twenty-four ships were wood sided. They carried a powerful collection of two hundred guns. These ships burned coal to make steam so that their paddle wheels revolved, or turned. The motion of the revolving paddle wheels moved the ships. In addition, the Union had nineteen mortar boats. Each carried one giant mortar, a type of short cannon. Sixty-one-year-old Admiral David Farragut commanded the entire fleet. Commander David Porter led the mortar boats and reported to Farragut.

The Fall of New Orleans

On April 18, 1862, the mortar boats began to fire at the forts. Their job was to destroy Fort St. Philip's and Fort Jackson's guns so the Union ships could move toward New Orleans. Union officers thought that the mortars would force the Confederates to surrender. But after a week of firing, Farragut saw that the mortars were doing little damage.

Farragut decided to lead his fleet past the forts anyway. He chose to make his try at 2:00 A.M. on April 24. A tremendous firefight, or gun battle, took place. The forts fired again and again. The ships fired back. The mortar boats opened fire. Small rebel boats pushed rafts heaped with burning wood into the path of the Union ships. The battle looked like a mighty display of fireworks. A Union officer wrote: "There were many fire-rafts, and these and the flashing of the guns and bursting shells [explosives] made it almost as light as day, but the smoke from the passing fleet was so thick that at times one could see nothing ten feet from the ship."

The naval battle was wild but short. A

Admiral David G. Farragut, above, *was one of the great naval leaders of the war. He had joined the navy at the age of nine.*

44

Confederate ram (a type of ship that attacks other ships by running into them) sank one Union ship. Three small Union boats had to turn back. The rest of Farragut's ships kept moving toward New Orleans through a gap in the chain barrier.

The much more powerful Union fleet destroyed the rebel fleet. By dawn on April 24, Farragut's ships had passed the forts. Thirty-six Union sailors died and 135 were wounded during the fighting.

Farragut captured New Orleans on April 25, 1862. This was a great Northern victory. The South had lost its largest city and most important port (place where trading ships can load and unload goods). Union forces held the city for the rest of the Civil War.

Farragut's victory at New Orleans allowed Union forces to enter the Mississippi River from the south. Farragut prepared to take his fleet north up the Mississippi River. Meanwhile, a Union fleet was fighting its way south on the Mississippi, from Kentucky toward Tennessee.

A Union mortar boat. The short, large gun shot high into the air, so that a shell could fly over the walls of a fort and land inside.

45

On to Memphis

The Confederate fort at Columbus, Kentucky, guarded the upper Mississippi River. The rebels had left this fort in February 1862 because Grant had moved against Fort Henry and Fort Donelson. The next rebel fort was fifty miles south on the Mississippi River. It was called Island No. 10. Union Flag Officer Andrew Foote used mortar boats to fire at Island No. 10. But, just as in New Orleans, the mortars did little damage.

A Union army commanded by General John Pope surrounded Island No. 10 on three sides. The Mississippi River flowed along the fourth side. Pope asked the Union navy to send an ironclad past the island to help him completely surround the fort. A fort was dangerous only when its guns could shoot at targets nearby. After a ship moved past the guns, it was safe. The ship could then control all of the area past the fort.

The ironclad waited until the night of April 4, 1862. A heavy thunderstorm helped to hide the

Union mortar boats bombard Island No. 10.

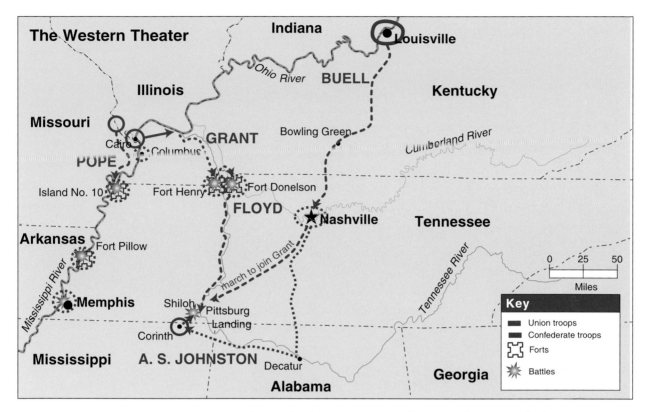

The Western Theater

Indiana

Louisville

Ohio River

BUELL

Illinois

Kentucky

Missouri

GRANT

Bowling Green

Cumberland River

Cairo

Columbus

POPE

Island No. 10

Fort Henry

Fort Donelson

FLOYD

Nashville

Tennessee

Arkansas

Fort Pillow

Mississippi River

march to join Grant

Tennessee River

Memphis

Shiloh

Pittsburg Landing

Corinth

Mississippi

A. S. JOHNSTON

Decatur

Alabama

Georgia

0   25   50

Miles

Key

Union troops
Confederate troops
Forts
Battles

ironclad as it moved past the Confederate guns. Two nights later another ironclad used another storm to pass the island. The two ironclads allowed Pope to surround Island No. 10. On April 7, the fort surrendered. Pope captured 7,000 Confederate soldiers along with valuable equipment and fifty-four guns. Pope became a new Northern hero.

The Union fleet continued south, downstream. Fifty miles north of Memphis, Tennessee, was Fort Pillow. The fort had forty guns. Eight rebel steamboats guarded the river. The Confederates had made these boats into rams. On May 10, 1862, they launched a surprise attack against the Union fleet. They rammed and sank two Union ironclads.

The success gave confidence to the Confederate sailors. The Southern fleet commander boasted that the Yankees "will never penetrate farther down the Mississippi." He was wrong.

Another Northern inventor-engineer came onto the scene. His name was Charles Ellet. Ellet believed that rams made the most powerful ships. He thought that rams worked especially well on rivers. So he designed and built an entire fleet made up of rams.

Ellet's chance came on June 6, 1862, at the Battle of Memphis. His rams were with the Union ironclads, heading south toward Memphis. They heard a cannon shot. Ellet shouted out, "It is a gun from the enemy! Round out and follow me! Now is our chance." Ellet's rams sank or damaged most of the Confederate fleet. The Union navy went on to capture Memphis, the South's fifth largest city.

Farragut's victory at New Orleans had opened the lower Mississippi to Union ships. The Union victory at Memphis opened the upper Mississippi. Only one more Confederate strong-hold, or series of forts, remained. It was at Vicksburg, Mississippi.

Union Defeat at Vicksburg

The Union navy moved toward Vicksburg from both the north and the south. Farragut's fleet

Battle of Memphis

arrived first on May 18, 1862. The Vicksburg defenses had many heavy guns dug into a hill along the river. Union naval officers thought the defenses were too strong for them to attack. So a Union captain tried a bluff, or trick.

He knew that the Union forces were too weak to capture Vicksburg. Still, he demanded that the city surrender. The mayor of Vicksburg replied, "Mississippians don't know, and refuse to learn, how to surrender. If Commodore Farragut . . . can teach them, let them come and try."

The Union ships alone could not capture Vicksburg. They needed infantry to complete the job. While the Union leaders were trying to figure out what to do, the Confederates made another surprise attack. This time it came from a rebel ironclad named the *Arkansas*.

The commander of the *Arkansas*, Isaac Brown, was an especially bold man who was willing to take risks. Brown decided to attack the Union fleet. It was one ship against many. The *Arkansas* fired at the Union ships as it moved toward Vicksburg. One by one the Union ships fired back. Some of the shots broke through the *Arkansas*'s armor.

A Confederate lieutenant described what it was like on the *Arkansas*. "I found myself standing in a dense, suffocating smoke, with my cap gone and hair and beard singed [burned]. The smoke soon cleared away, and I found one man left. Sixteen men were killed and wounded by that shell, and the ship set on fire."

The damaged *Arkansas* limped past the Union ships and stopped at Vicksburg. Its attack proved that the Confederates would defend Vicksburg with great determination. Union leaders knew that they needed infantry to help them, so Union ships withdrew from Vicksburg. But they would return the next year.

The CSS Arkansas *running through the Union fleet near Vicksburg*

CHAPTER FIVE

Fighting in Kentucky and Mississippi

>⊹>─○─<⊹<

A fter the Battle of Shiloh, General Braxton Bragg replaced General Pierre Beauregard as commander of the Confederate Army of Tennessee. This army was the main Confederate army in the west. Bragg made a new plan. Two small forces stayed in western Tennessee. Their job was to stop General Grant's Union army. Meanwhile, Bragg moved most of his men east by train. They gathered at Chattanooga, Tennessee, and planned to strike north into Union-controlled Kentucky.

The campaign became known as "Bragg's Invasion of Kentucky." It began on July 20, 1862. By the middle of September, the Confederates controlled much of Kentucky. The Confederate leaders thought that many Kentucky men would join their armies. They were disappointed when very few Kentuckians joined him. Bragg said, "The people here have too many fat cattle and are too well off to fight."

Still, the tide seemed to be shifting in favor of the Confederacy. In the east, Confederate General Robert E. Lee was invading the North. In the west, Bragg was in Kentucky. September 1862 proved to be a critical time. If the South could win a few more victories, it had a good chance to win the Civil War.

But in Kentucky, Bragg was unable to cooperate, or work with, the commander of a nearby Confederate army. Their failure to work as a team meant that each army went off on its own.

A battery is a group of soldiers in charge of large guns such as cannons. Here a Confederate battery is shown with their guns.

Confederate General Braxton Bragg

On the morning of October 8, 1862, a confused fight began near the town of Perryville, Kentucky, between Bragg's Confederate army and General Buell's Union army. The weather was hot and dry. No rain had fallen for a long time. The battle began because both armies were looking for drinking water. It was fought with typical western stubbornness. By nightfall, the Union suffered 4,211 casualties (soldiers who are killed, wounded, or missing). The Confederates suffered 3,396 casualties.

Bragg ordered a retreat. The Confederate march back south did not end until the army had left Kentucky. Bragg's Invasion of Kentucky ended in failure for the South.

Grant in Mississippi

During the time of Bragg's Invasion of Kentucky, Grant's Union army was in western Tennessee. His job had two parts. He had to guard the railroads of western Tennessee because trains brought supplies to Union forces. He also had to

NAMING AN ARMY

Civil War armies had names. Union armies usually took their names from the name of a river. The biggest, most famous Union army in the east was the Army of the Potomac. It was named after the Potomac River that flowed near Washington, D.C. In the west, General Ulysses S. Grant's army was the Army of the Tennessee, and General William S. Rosecrans's army was the Army of the Cumberland. These two Union armies were named after the Tennessee River and the Cumberland River, which both flow through the state of Tennessee.

Confederate armies usually took their names from a state or an area. In the east, General Robert E. Lee's army was called the Army of Northern Virginia. In the west, General Braxton Bragg's army was called the Army of Tennessee.

send reinforcements to help defend Kentucky. Then the Confederates attacked him once again.

The most important battle took place at Corinth, Mississippi, just south of the Tennessee border, on October 3 and 4 in 1862. The key position at Corinth was a type of fort called an earthwork. Soldiers made the earthwork by digging a trench and piling up dirt. The earthwork gave the Union soldiers protection from Confederate musket and artillery fire. The rebels charged with great courage but could not capture the earthwork. The result was a Confederate defeat.

At the time, the Battle of Corinth seemed to be just another fight. In fact, it was much more. Union General William T. Sherman explained the battle's importance for the North: "It was indeed, a decisive blow to the Confederate cause

Battle of Corinth

in our [area], and changed the whole [war] in West Tennessee. From the timid defensive [waiting for the rebels to attack] we were at once enabled to assume the bold offensive [able to attack the rebels]."

For the rest of the war, Grant would be on the offensive, or moving to attack the Confederates. After the Battle of Corinth, his first goal was to take Vicksburg. The campaign to capture Vicksburg would be long and difficult.

The End of 1862

There were two ways for Grant to move his army toward Vicksburg. One was by moving by ship down the Mississippi River. But this was difficult because Confederate batteries, or groups of large guns, protected the river at Vicksburg. The second way was to march by land. The best route was to march south along the line of the Mississippi Central Railroad.

The Confederates had wrecked this railroad by burning the bridges. Grant figured that his soldiers could fix the railroad as they advanced. The railroad could then supply his army with food and ammunition.

The Confederate commander at Vicksburg was John Pemberton. Pemberton was a Northerner who had married a Southern woman. When the Civil War began, Pemberton volunteered for the Southern army. Still, many Southerners distrusted their "Yankee" general. One Confederate complained, "Oh what will our Country come to, when we are cursed with such worthless Commanders."

Confederate General John Pemberton, joined the Confederate army in spite of the fact that his two brothers had joined the Union army.

President Davis liked and trusted Pemberton. Davis told the governor of Mississippi that Pemberton was "an officer of great merit [skill]." Pemberton badly wanted to earn the trust of the Southern people. He believed that the best way to do this was to defend Vicksburg against the Union.

Pemberton understood the importance of the Mississippi Central Railroad. He sent General Earl Van Dorn with a cavalry force to raid the railroad, burn bridges, and destroy trains. Van Dorn's cavalry surprised the Union soldiers at Holly Spring, Mississippi, about 190 miles northeast of Vicksburg. The rebel cavalry routed the Union soldiers (made them run away) and destroyed Grant's supplies.

The loss of supplies convinced Grant to change his strategy. He decided he could not advance against Vicksburg by marching down the railroad. He would have to use the Mississippi River to attack Vicksburg. But first his army needed food.

Grant ordered his men to take food and supplies from the nearby farms and large estates called plantations. In times of war, this is called living off of the land. In times of peace, it is called stealing.

Union soldier with rifle, musket, and bayonet. His equipment is next to him, including a blanket, a knapsack, and a canteen.

Grant's soldiers found that they could take all that they needed from people's farms. This surprised Grant. He later wrote: "This taught me a lesson." Grant learned that most of the time his army needed a secure supply line. In other words, most often it had to stay near a railroad or a river. But for a short time, for special missions, it could live off the local people.

After gathering food, Grant marched his army to the Mississippi River. Meanwhile, different Union forces tried to capture Vicksburg. General William T. Sherman commanded the army infantry. David Porter, who had been promoted to admiral, commanded the navy fleet. Sherman and Porter worked well together.

A Union flag-bearer, opposite. During a battle, soldiers followed their flag and fought to protect it. The soldier carrying the flag was easy for the enemy to see and often got shot.

After their victory at Memphis, Tennessee, Union navy ironclads steamed south down the Mississippi River, below.

Porter's fleet carried Sherman's men to a place just north of Vicksburg on the east bank of the Mississippi River. The news came to Vicksburg on December 24, 1862. It was Christmas Eve. Most of the Confederate officers were at a holiday ball, or dance. A muddy messenger entered the ballroom. A Confederate general asked, "Well sir, what do you want?" The messenger told him that the Union forces were coming. The general turned pale. He said in a loud voice, "This ball is at an end." The Confederate soldiers rushed to protect Vicksburg.

Sherman's men had to advance through a swamp known as Chickasaw Bayou. There were only a few routes through the swamp. All led straight into Confederate earthworks and trenches. Sherman said, "We will lose 5,000 men before we take Vicksburg, and may as well lose them here as anywhere else." He ordered the advance on December 29, 1862.

A Union officer described the scene as the Union soldiers waited for the order to charge the Confederate earthworks: "I noticed various faces that almost visibly changed and got paler and paler. The eyes looked so hollow.... And the hand gripped the rifle... and believed that they had found their own rescuer in that. Others looked terribly solemn [thoughtful] and seemed impatient for the moment when they could sacrifice themselves. Still others, and so it was with me, were determined, pressed their lips together and stared at our flag."

The Union charge was a total, bloody failure. Sherman's men retreated. They blamed Sherman for the attack's failure. An Iowa captain wrote to his wife about "a useless sacrifice of life" and how "our Generals do not understand their business and do not appear to care for the loss of life no more than were we so many brutes [animals]."

CHAPTER SIX

"A Hard Earned Victory": The Battle of Stones River

Union General William Starke Rosecrans was born in Ohio and graduated from the U.S. Military Academy at West Point. Before the Civil War, he had worked as an engineer.

While the Union forces struggled to take Vicksburg, two powerful armies faced one another in central Tennessee. General Bragg was still in command of the Confederate Army of Tennessee. His men were a little discouraged after their retreat from Kentucky. But they could blame their failure on the people of Kentucky. After all, Kentucky men had failed to join the Confederate army. The Confederates had failed to conquer Kentucky, but they had few doubts that they could defend Tennessee, which was part of the Confederacy.

General William S. Rosecrans was commander of a Union force that had a new name: the Army of the Cumberland. Rosecrans was good at making plans. He was brave. But sometimes he became too excited during a battle. At such times he did not think clearly. Still, his men liked him. They called him "Old Rosey."

On December 26, 1862, Rosecrans left his base at Nashville, Tennessee, and marched his army south. Bragg decided to stand and fight at the town of Murfreesboro, Tennessee. On the night of December 30, the two armies faced each other outside of Murfreesboro. Bragg commanded about 38,000 Confederate soldiers. Rosecrans commanded a slightly larger force of about 45,000 Union soldiers.

The only way to stay warm was to huddle close to a fire during the very cold night before the Battle of Stones River. Some officers ordered their men not to build fires so that the enemy soldiers could not see them.

During the night, Rosecrans and Bragg each gave orders to attack the enemy when morning came. A small river called Stones River flowed just to the east of the Union army camp. Rosecrans planned to cross Stones River to attack the Confederate's right flank. Bragg, meanwhile, planned to attack the Union army's right flank. Since most of Bragg's men did not have to cross the river, they struck first.

The battle took place on flat ground. There were many small cedar thickets (groups of trees). The cedar trees made it hard for soldiers to see far. More important, the Union leaders failed to make sure that their men were ready for a battle. This failure meant that the rebel attack came as a surprise to the Union army.

At first it was just like it had been at Shiloh. A rebel charge came out from behind the trees. The Confederates struck the Union soldiers in their camps. A Union soldier described the scene: "I could hear the bullets striking the [corn]stalks. I could hear them strike a comrade as he ran. Then there would be a groan, a stagger, and a fall. I could hear the wild yelling behind, and the roar

The Battle of Stones River, above, *was the first big fight for many soldiers.*

Union General Philip Sheridan, below, *was put in charge of a cavalry unit in 1862. Then he became a great battle leader of both infantry and cavalry.*

of guns. . . . I saw the fields . . . filling up with regiments and columns and armies of gray [the color of Confederate soldiers' uniforms]. . . . I felt as though I would like to be all legs, with no other purpose in life but to run."

Union soldiers fought hard and slowed the Confederate advance. Philip Sheridan, who commanded a Union infantry division, showed especially good leadership. But the Confederates slowly fought their way around the Union right flank. This forced the Union men to retreat.

Rosecrans rode among his men to rally, or encourage, them. A cannonball tore apart one of his aides. The dying man's blood splattered on Rosecrans's uniform. The general ignored it. He worked furiously to regain control of the fight.

Meanwhile, the Confederates attacked the Union line again and again. At one place, the rebels charged across an old cotton field. The noise of the fight was so loud that men paused. They grabbed some cotton to stuff in their ears. Then they charged again.

Bragg's army forced Rosecrans's army back to Stones River. One more try and the Confederates would have won the battle. But the fighting had lasted ten hours and the rebels were exhausted. Many soldiers had no more ammunition. Others had simply run out of strength. A Confederate general wrote: "My men had had little or no rest the night before; they had been fighting since dawn, without relief, food, or water."

A cold winter night came. Few soldiers had any shelter. Many of the wounded were left lying on the battlefield. They suffered terribly. An Ohio

Union General Rosecrans acted bravely during the Battle of Stones River.

soldier wrote: "Men were wounded in every [possible] way, some with their arms shot off, some wounded in the body, some in the head."

Bragg's army had almost won the battle. Bragg felt certain that Rosecrans would retreat. Bragg decided to wait until the Union army left the battlefield. Then he would claim victory for his Confederate army.

Rosecrans met with his generals. Everyone was tired. Some were discouraged. But Rosecrans insisted that the army stay where it was. He ordered his soldiers to defend the ground where they had stood at the end of the first day of battle. During the night he reorganized his army. Stragglers (men who had left the fight) returned during the night, ready to fight the next day. Union morale, or spirits, rose.

Bragg was surprised to see the Union army still in position. New Year's Day 1863 passed quietly. On January 2, a part of Bragg's army made another attack. It also failed to drive off the Union army. This failure convinced Bragg that he had to retreat. On the night of January 3, his army marched back south to Alabama.

Both armies had fought very hard. The battle cost each army about 12,000 men. The South suffered more from the losses because they had fewer soldiers than the North.

In the end, Stones River became a battle between the generals. Each was stubborn. Neither Rosecrans nor Bragg wanted to retreat. Bragg gave up first. The Confederate retreat made Stones River a Union victory.

The victory came at an important time. The

Northern people were becoming tired of the war. Union people living in states such as Illinois and Michigan were talking about making peace. The victory at Stones River helped some people believe that the Union could win the Civil War.

The newspapers helped to encourage them. The *Chicago Tribune* reported the battle on January 6, 1863. The headline read: "Rosecrans Wins a Complete Victory; the Enemy in Full Retreat."

President Lincoln understood how the Union victory gave some Northerners hope. He wrote to Rosecrans: "I can never forget...you gave us a

The Battle of Stones River, near Murfreesboro, Tennessee, was an important Union victory.

hard earned victory, which, had there been a defeat instead, the nation could scarcely have lived."

Looking Back at 1862

When Southerners looked back at the events of 1862, they rejoiced at Confederate victories in the west. Pemberton had defeated Sherman at Chickasaw Bayou. And Bragg had at least stopped the Union advance in Tennessee.

Most Northern people looked back at 1862 and found little to make them happy. Sherman had been defeated outside of Vicksburg. The Battle of Stones River was a good victory, but afterward Rosecrans's army was too badly hurt to move.

Northerners were very unhappy with Grant. They knew that Grant had won some victories, but he had made little progress since the end of May. The *New York Times* wrote, "Grant remains stuck in the mud of northern Mississippi, his army for weeks of no use to him or to anybody else." Ohio's *Cincinnati Commercial* was even angrier. It declared that Grant had done nothing for a long time. He had "botched [made serious mistakes in] the whole campaign." The newspaper's editor had powerful friends inside the Lincoln government. This man told his friends that Grant was a fool, a drunk, and a threat to the nation. It seemed that Lincoln might remove Grant from command of the Union army in Tennessee.

Then early in 1863, winter rains flooded the Mississippi River area. Movement anywhere was almost impossible. Grant thought about retreating north until the land dried out. Instead, he decided to keep trying to capture Vicksburg. He clearly said what he wanted: "to go forward to a decisive [important] victory." As soon as the land dried out, Grant's decisive campaign would begin.

A Civil War Navy

How a Navy Was Organized

During the Civil War, the Union and the Confederacy each had their own navy. But the Union navy was always much bigger than the Confederate navy. The navies fought on the Atlantic Ocean and on American rivers, such as the Mississippi River.

A navy is completely separate from an army. It has separate officers (leaders), separate weapons, and separate fighting men called sailors. But often a navy and an army worked together to win a battle.

Rank is the level of job held by a soldier or a sailor. An admiral is the highest ranking officer in a navy. The ranks under admiral are commodore, captain, commander, lieutenant commander, lieutenant, master, and ensign. Cadets (students) who have just graduated from the U.S. Naval Academy at Annapolis, Maryland, are called midshipmen. Sailors are also given names because of the jobs they do on ships. Some examples from the Civil War are gunner, carpenter's mate, painter, and ship's cook.

Civil War sailors lived on their ships. They slept in hammocks that they hung up each night and took down each morning. Their daily diet included salted meat, biscuit (hard bread), beans or peas, cheese, and coffee or tea. Every day sailors cleaned the whole ship. They also practiced skills needed during a naval battle, such as firing cannons or putting out fires. On weekends they had to repair and wash their clothing. Sailors were sometimes allowed to go ashore for a short time when their ships stopped at a port (city near an ocean or river) for supplies or repairs.

How a Navy Moved

Ships that fought on rivers had to be built differently than ships that fought on the ocean. River boats were narrower and sat higher in the water, so that most of the ship floated above the water. With only a small part of the ship underwater, a river boat could go through shallow water or narrow passages without getting stuck.

Most ships in the Civil War used steam power, which was the best way to move ships at that time. Steam engines burned large amounts of coal or wood to heat water, which made steam. The steam then turned either a paddle wheel or a propeller, which moved the ship through the water. The Union and Confederate navies also had a few sailing ships, which used wind to move.

How a Navy Fought

The Union and Confederate navies had several kinds of ships. They had warships, which carried big cannons. Both navies had ironclads. These ships were covered with iron plates called armor, which protected them from enemy gunfire. Both sides also used rams, which were ships fitted with a

powerful engine and a sharp pole on the front end. A ram would run into an enemy ship, punch a hole in it, and cause the enemy ship to sink. The Union navy had mortar boats that they used in river battles. A mortar boat was a raft that held a mortar (a large, short cannon) hidden behind an ironclad wall.

The Confederate navy also invented and built a new type of boat: a submarine. These small, steam-powered crafts moved mostly underwater, but their smokestacks showed above the surface.

The Union and Confederate navies both used the newest naval inventions on their ships. Steam-powered revolving gun turrets (towers) allowed a ship to shoot in any direction without having to turn the whole ship. Torpedoes, or underwater explosives, could be placed in the water near an enemy ship or left in a river to blow up a passing enemy ship.

The CSS Hunley, *an example of the newly invented submarines, blew up a Union ship by sneaking up to it and planting a torpedo near it. On its way back to port, the* Hunley *sank for unknown reasons, and the entire crew drowned.*

Ships were used to stop other ships from traveling on rivers and on the ocean. This is called a blockade. For example, during the Civil War, the Union navy blockaded the South by preventing Southern ships from entering or leaving Southern ports. This kept the South from selling cotton or buying food and other supplies. Southern ships, called blockade runners, tried to get in and out of seaports by sneaking past the Union navy ships. At the beginning of the war, one out of ten blockade runners got caught by Union ships while trying to get through the blockade. By the end of the war, six hundred Union ships took part in the blockade. By then, one out of every three blockade runners was caught by the Union navy.

Time Line

September 3, 1861: Confederate troops take control of Columbus, Kentucky, even though Kentucky is a neutral state in the Civil War.

September 5, 1861: Two days after Confederate troops move into Kentucky, Union troops take control of Paducah, Kentucky.

February 6, 1862: Union ironclad ships move down the Tennessee River and capture Fort Henry, Tennessee, from the Confederates.

February 16, 1862: General Ulysses S. Grant receives the "unconditional surrender" of Fort Donelson, Tennessee, from the Confederates.

April 6–7, 1862: Battle of Shiloh. The Confederates, led by General Albert Sidney Johnston, make a surprise attack and almost defeat General Grant's Union army while it is camped in Tennessee near the Tennessee River.

April 7, 1862: The Union army and navy work together to capture Confederate Island No. 10 on the Mississippi River.

April 25, 1862: Union Admiral David Farragut captures New Orleans, Louisiana.

June 6, 1862: Battle of Memphis. The Union navy defeats the Confederate navy and captures Memphis, Tennessee.

October 3–4, 1862: Battle of Corinth. The Union defeats the Confederate attack against the railroad center at Corinth, Mississippi.

October 8, 1862: Battle of Perryville, Kentucky. The Union just barely manages to win.

December 29, 1862: Battle of Chickasaw Bayou. The Confederates defeat Union troops at Chickasaw Bayou, Mississippi, outside of Vicksburg.

December 31, 1862–January 2, 1863: Battle of Stones River, Tennessee. Again, the Union just barely wins.

Notes

For quoted material in text:

p. 14, William C. Davis, *Jefferson Davis: The Man and His Hour* (New York: HarperCollins Publishers, 1991), 396.

p. 21, Benjamin Franklin Cooling, *Forts Henry and Donelson: The Key to the Confederate Heartland* (Knoxville, TN: University of Tennessee Press, 1987), 116.

p. 23, Letter of Charles Sackett to his mother, 12th Iowa Infantry, Fort Donelson National Military Park, Dover, TN.

p. 24, *Battles and Leaders of the Civil War* (New York: Thomas Yoseloff, 1956), 1: 433.

p. 27, Bruce Catton, *Grant Moves South* (Boston: Little, Brown and Co., 1960), 165.

p. 28, Wiley Sword, *Shiloh: Bloody April* (Dayton, OH: Morningside Bookshop, 1988), 155.

p. 29, From the National Park Service markers at Fort Donelson National Military Park, Dover, TN.

p. 29, Ibid.

p. 31, Catton, *Grant Moves South*, 175.

p. 32, *Battles and Leaders of the Civil War*, 1: 550.

p. 32, Davis, *Jefferson Davis*, 398.

p. 35, Sword, *Shiloh*, 148.

p. 35, James R. Arnold, *The Armies of U.S. Grant* (London: Arms and Armour Press, 1995), 60.

p. 36, Byron R. Abernethy, ed., *Private Elisha Stockwell, Jr. Sees the Civil War* (Norman, OK: University of Oklahoma Press, 1958), 60.

p. 37, James R. Arnold, *Shiloh 1862: The Death of Innocence* (Oxford: Osprey Publishing, 1998), 54.

p. 38, Henry Villiard, *Memoirs of Henry Villiard* (Boston: Houghton Mifflin Co., 1904), 1: 244.

p. 41, T. Harry Williams, *Lincoln and His Generals* (New York: Alfred A. Knopf, 1952), 86.

p. 41, James R. Arnold, *Presidents Under Fire: Commanders in Chief in Victory and Defeat* (New York: Orion Books, 1994), 151.

p. 44, *Battles and Leaders of the Civil War* (New York: Thomas Yoseloff, 1956), 2: 63.

p. 47, Report of Captain Montgomery, 12 May 1862, in *Official Records of the Union and Confederate Navies in the War of the Rebellion*, ser. 1, vol. 23 (Washington, DC: Government Printing Office, 1910), 57.

p. 48, Edwin C. Bearss, *Hardluck Ironclad: The Sinking and Salvage of the* Cairo (Baton Rouge, LA: Louisiana State University Press, 1966), 72.

p. 49, Letter from the military governor of Vicksburg, 18 May 1862, in *Official Records of the Union and Confederate Navies in the War of the Rebellion*, ser. 1, vol. 18 (Washington, DC: Government Printing Office, 1904), 492.

p. 49, George W. Gift, "The Story of the *Arkansas*," *Southern Historical Society Papers*, vol. 12, no. 3, pt. 2 (March 1884), 117.

p. 50, Peter Cozzens, *No Better Place to Die: The Battle of Stones River* (Chicago: University of Illinois Press, 1990), 6.

p. 53, William Tecumseh Sherman, *Memoirs of General W. T. Sherman* (New York: Library of America, 1990), 284.

p. 54, Bell Irvin Wiley, ed., *"This Infernal War": The Confederate Letters of Sgt. Edwin H. Fay* (Austin, TX: University of Texas Press, 1958), 179.

p. 55, Jefferson Davis to John Pettus, 30 September 1862, in *War of the Rebellion: Official Records of the Union and Confederate Armies*, ser. 1, vol. 17, pt. 2 (Washington, DC: Government Printing Office, 1890), 716.

p. 56, Ulysses S. Grant, *Personal Memoirs* (New York: Da Capo Press, 1982), 226.

p. 57, Stephen D. Lee, "Details of Important Work Done by Two Confederate Telegraph Operators, Christmas Eve, 1862," *Publications of the Mississippi Historical Society*, vol. 8 (1904), 54.

p. 57, Ibid.

p. 57, *Battles and Leaders of the Civil War* (New York: Thomas Yoseloff, 1956), 3: 467.

p. 57, Earl J. Hess, ed., *A German in the Yankee Fatherland: The Civil War Letters of Henry A. Kircher* (Kent, OH: Kent State University Press, 1983), 47.

p. 57, Florence Cox, ed., *Kiss Josey For Me!* (Santa Ana, CA: Friis-Pioneer Press, 1974), 116.

p. 57, Ibid.

p. 59, Richard Wheeler, *Voices of the Civil War* (New York: Thomas Y. Crowell Company, 1976), 229.

p. 60, Cozzens, *No Better Place to Die*, 150.

p. 61, Ibid., 171.

p. 62, Roy P. Basler, ed., *The Collected Works of Abraham Lincoln* (New Brunswick, NJ: Rutgers University Press, 1953), 6: 424.

p. 63, "News of the Day: The Operation Against Vicksburgh," *New York Times*, 12 January 1863, p. 4.

p. 63, Arnold, *The Armies of U.S. Grant*, 94.

p. 63, Grant, *Personal Memoirs*, 231.

For quoted material in sidebars:

p. 12, Arnold, *The Armies of U.S. Grant*, 9.

>─┤◆>─○─<◆├─<

Selected Bibliography

Arnold, James R. *The Armies of U.S. Grant*. London: Arms and Armour Press, 1995.

Battles and Leaders of the Civil War. Vols. 1, 2, and 3. New York: Thomas Yoseloff, 1956.

Boatner, Mark Mayo, III. *The Civil War Dictionary*. New York: David McKay Co., 1959.

Catton, Bruce. *Grant Moves South*. Boston: Little, Brown and Co., 1960.

Cozzens, Peter. *No Better Place to Die: The Battle of Stones River*. Chicago: University of Illinois Press, 1990.

Davis, William C. *Jefferson Davis: The Man and His Hour*. New York: HarperCollins Publishers, 1991.

Esposito, Vincent J., ed. *The West Point Atlas of American Wars*. Vol. 1. New York: Frederick A. Praeger Publishers, 1959.

Grant, Ulysses S. *Personal Memoirs*. 1885. Reprint, New York: Da Capo Press, 1982.

Sword, Wiley. *Shiloh: Bloody April*. Dayton, OH: Morningside Bookshop, 1988.

Williams, T. Harry. *Lincoln and His Generals*. New York: Alfred A. Knopf, 1952.

For More Information

Books
Burchard, Peter. *Lincoln and Slavery*. New York: Atheneum, 1999.

Clinton, Catherine. *Scholastic Encyclopedia of the Civil War*. New York: Scholastic, Inc., 1999.

Day, Nancy. *Your Travel Guide to Civil War America*. Minneapolis: Runestone Press, 2001.

Dolan, Edward F. *The American Civil War: A House Divided*. Brookfield, CT: Millbrook Press, 1997.

Freedman, Russell. *Lincoln: A Photobiography*. New York: Clarion Books, 1987.

Grabowski, Patricia. *Robert E. Lee*. Philadelphia: Chelsea House, 2000.

Hakim, Joy. *War, Terrible War*. New York: Oxford University Press, 1994.

January, Brendan. *The Emancipation Proclamation*. New York: Children's Press, 1997.

Marrin, Albert. *Unconditional Surrender: U.S. Grant and the Civil War*. New York: Atheneum, 1994.

Ransom, Candace. *Children of the Civil War*. Minneapolis: Carolrhoda Books, 1998.

Savage, Douglas J. *The Civil War in the West*. New York: Chelsea House, 2000.

Shorto, Russell. *David Farragut and the Great Naval Blockade*. Englewood Cliffs, NJ: Silver Burdett Press, 1991.

Smith, Carter, ed. *The First Battles: A Sourcebook on the Civil War*. Brookfield, CT: Millbrook Press, 1993.

Stanchak, John. *Civil War*. New York: Dorling Kindersley, 2000.

Steins, Richard. *Shiloh*. New York: Twenty-First Century Books, 1997.

Video
The Civil War. Walpole, NH: Florentine Films, 1990. Videocassette series. This PBS series by Ken Burns and narrated by David McCullough includes personal accounts and archival photos, as well as commentary by many writers on the period.

Civil War Journal. New York: A & E Networks, 1993. Videocassette series. Includes diaries and reenactments.

Web Sites
<http://www.ajkids.com>
> Users can ask questions about U.S. history in plain language and get connected to several different sites with answers.

<http://memory.loc.gov/ammem/cwphtml/cwphome.html>
> Users can view the Selected Civil War Photographs Collection of the Library of Congress.

Places to Visit
Fort Donelson National Battlefield , Dover, Tennessee, has 537 acres and a trail along the river to the place where Confederate guns repelled the Union ironclads.

Shiloh National Military Park, Shiloh, Tennessee, has 3,838 well-preserved acres and a great artillery collection.

Stones River National Battlefield, Murfreesboro, Tennessee, has 405 acres, and visitors can see where the Union soldiers placed artillery.

Index

A Union battle line with a second line in reserve at the Battle of Stones River

About the Authors

James R. Arnold was born in Illinois, and his family moved to Switzerland when he was a teenager. His fascination with the history of war was born on the battlefields of Europe. He returned to the United States for his college education. For the past twenty-five years, he and his wife, Roberta Wiener, have lived and farmed in the Shenandoah Valley of Virginia and toured all the Civil War battlefields.

Mr. Arnold's great-great-grandfather was shot and killed in Fairfax, Virginia, because he voted against secession. Another ancestor served in an Ohio regiment during the Civil War. Mr. Arnold has written more than twenty books about American and European wars, and he has contributed to many others.

Roberta Wiener grew up in Pennsylvania and completed her education in Washington, D.C. After many years of touring battlefields and researching books with her husband, James R. Arnold, she has said, "The more I learn about war, the more fascinating it becomes." Ms. Wiener has coauthored nine books with Mr. Arnold and edited numerous educational books, including a children's encyclopedia. She has also worked as an archivist for the U.S. Army.

>━►━○━◄━<

Picture Acknowledgments

Author photo: 16, 20, 24, 29, 30B, 31. Frank Leslie's Illustrated Newspaper: 13, 16-17, 28, 34. Library of Congress: 6-7, 9, 14R, 15, 20-21, 22, 26-27, 30T, 32-33, 36B, 40-41, 41T, 46, 50-51, 52, 53, 54, 59, 61, 62-63, 70-71. National Archives: 6, 8, 10-11, 23, 24-25, 35T, 35B, 36T, 44, 45, 55, 57T, 58, 60B. *Plenty of Fighting today: The 9th Illinois at Shiloh,"* a National Guard Heritage painting by Keith Rocco, courtesy of the National Guard bureau, 40T, Naval Historical Center, Washington, D.C.: 18, 18-19, 19T, 42-43, 48, 49, 56-57, 65. West Point Museum Collection, U.S. Military Academy: title page, 14TL, 14BL, 38-39. U.S. Naval Academy Museum, Beverley R. Robinson Collection: front cover, U.S. Signal Corps: back cover, *"Baptism by Fire,"* by Robert W. Wilson, Woodruff, SC 60T.

Maps by Jerry Malone